My First

Craig Balmer

BookLeaf Publishing

India | USA | UK

My First Words © 2023 Craig Balmer

All rights reserved.

No part of this publication may be
reproduced, stored in a retrieval system, or
transmitted, in any form or by any means,
electronic, mechanical, photocopying,
recording or otherwise, without the prior
written permission of the presenters.

Craig Balmer asserts the moral right to be
identified as author of this work.

Presentation by *BookLeaf Publishing*

Web: www.bookleafpub.com

E-mail: info@bookleafpub.com

ISBN: 9789358737370

First edition 2023

ACKNOWLEDGEMENT

To Sarah, Thankyou for the six words, this book would not be here without you.

And to Sylvia Plath, your words were a gold mine in a darkened time I have posthumously dug up. Anyone who knows me, knows!

And thanks to the Donny poetry folks who have listened to me over the years.

PREFACE

This book has been composed as part of a 21 day challenge. I would like to say every work in here is brand new. It is not. Work dictates that this has been quite the challenge. They are however, all freshly edited by myself. And some are very new. This book is part my renaissance. I have come to spit fire!

Extinction Events!

BOGOF! Sale is starting now
Buy before you die

Political thoughts
Thatcher in deed is a liar
Who are these people?

Jagger's Song

My first teacher was a cunt, her name was Mrs
Jagger,
No friend of Mick's or quite so slick she often
played the pianer.
As name suggests a churlish bitch, she was
really, quite the cunt.
If you so much as suggested this you were
treated like a runt.

She'd sit us down in whitened skids and tinkle
out a tune.
A nice doleful religious hit, pleasing all within
the room!
And then one day she played a banger and I
started to sing.
With great gusto and joyful bell my voice began
to ring,

But 'twas not for long, as class all as one, burst
out into laughter.
And I myself have never sung; there or
elsewhere after.
So, the class duly got admonished but not for
mocking me.

They got castigation for halted clunking of the keys.

So away from mumbled singing she'd often take a seat.
Have us all crossed legged, sat affront her sweaty feet.
Then she'd take to reading sitting in her hirsute skirt.
We sat upon the floorboards till our butts began to hurt.

Sat with her legs akimbo, we faced horrendous visions.
Nora Batty stockings covered hairy legs and linens.
The stories that unfolded were most likely never listened
For behind the hairy fabric a hairy monster glistened.

So, then I hold my hand up "Miss I need to go the toilet"
"What, really; now?" "Yes Miss, I really cannot hold it!"
So off it was I trotted with guts a grumbling and a rumbling,
I make it to the cubicle, all fingers; and my thumbs they are a fumbling.

Oh, by some twisted turn of fate and with pants drawn down to my thighs.

A giant pat comes tumbling out and splats neatly in my Y's.

I sat there overwhelmed, undies slumping to my ankles.

Letting out my little sobs, this was far more than I could handle!

And so, it was with teacher as she come bursting through the door!

"What the hell are y…" she stops; as jaw drops to the floor.

"Arghh, I cannot deal with that mess, you dirty, dirty little boy!"

Pants pulled up, marched back to class, along with foulest foy.

With temper foul, she sat me down, in my tiny little chair,

Wandered off with a frown and simply left me there.

And I sat wreaking, hair curling, squelched upon a seat.

Until the final bell I sat, when I could finally take my feet.

Off I shuffled, as you would, withholding what
there festered.
To meet my Mum, with her friend? (oh my God)
Sat in her green fiesta!
This was not the usual, two more jump in, I'm
squashed up in the middle!
Still, I sit, trying not to fiddle: yes, still I sit, as
foulest whiff, presents them with a riddle?

A sniff here, an accusing sniff there, a look
between them, and then a stare!
"I can smell shit!?" As they both look back with
an accusatory glare.
Dragged out the car, shorts unbound the source
of stench was quickly found.
"That's not fresh?" Glad of her friend, then
questions thrown, began to sound.
We are at this story' ending, and every day from
here on in my Mum would be attending.

My First Words

Excuse me Miss, could you explain to me this;
Where Do I put a Comma? And why Bother?
"You put it here!" So, she says, with some remiss,

                          And all a
pother.

No explanation, and that is it, dismissed.
She filters away to her favourite kids.
And I, left-handed, head smudging, scratching.
Missed

                          As a
Comma skids;

Anywhere I've put it! "Miss, I think I've done it!"
Incredulity comes o'er; she is not wrong.
"It is when you breath! Take a breath, then put it!"

                          Turns back to the
throng.

And so, I'm breathing, soft, hard; deep, and long, placed
Comma's everywher'n way, without correction

I put one here, one ear, literally laced

> Breath in,

perfection!

And out the other, alongside my perception,
that this would surely vex! Oh, so vexed indeed
At this lacking boy and this imperfection;

> A poorly

sewn seed.

Cast o'er broad bottom; Drowned in abysmal
Styx.
And it surely died, as schooling died, within
myself again, at age of tender six.

> So little learnt

therein.

Bleak House

I entered this world with bleak dismay.
Less a feeling more a knowing.
I dreamt of life one thousand dreams away.

Perhaps it was just the day to day
Lung draining, back slapping, chest blowing
Within this world so bleak, dismayed.

Rhythmical repression in twice daily sonic
waves.
Absorbing expulsion, without ever knowing.
I dreamed in life one thousand dreams away.

Percussive, sputum-spluttered: through walled
filtered haze.
Heart beat crushed with certain unknowing.
The endless world of bleak dismay's

Days spent within sonic solitary refinement rays.
Stochastic; measured pulses, slowly driven,
ingrowing.
Undreaming that life one thousand dreams away.

An impatient Sun arose behind sullen clouded
days.

Upon hearts that withered with a love,
un-glowing.
Entered, then left the world in bleak dismay
Alone with their dreams, one thousand dreams
away.

St. Wilfrid

I hated going to St. Wilfrid's place.
Dragged I was, along with morbid face,
But there was no bewailing.
For a mother's hand would come, flailing
If I, so much as muttered, discontent;
If one did not concede you would repent!
Beneath those ivory water towers.
Beyond the scabby Leylandii bowers.
It lay, pebble dashed, red door unlatched
And grey, one house but semi-detached,

From reality. We went through the door
Eighties carpet and a wailing score.
The bemoaning groans of What's'ername?!
Again, this time slumped against a frame.
Carpets match the jumper! A sickening sight
Which at times could be quite the fright.
Was she alright? She was not well,
But what was wrong I could not tell
You that secret feeling of disgust.
These were just not things that were discussed

My concerns, my growing sadness
Left to myself in this house of madness
In the cue behind the buffet killer!

What's'ername!? Dribbling into my potential
dinner.
Our Lee cluster sneezing upon every meal.
I just cannot tell you how ill I'd feel.
Fucking dribble and snot every which way.
And my fuck did he sneeze and every day.
But this is not how I should be!
I'm normal right I can just be me?

The Eye

That sight it left your eye that day,
as stone it flew with all my might.
I'm sorrier than I could ever say.
When it turned your day to night

Like a meteor in dreadful flight.
As darkness flew, you looked that way,
With awful flash of painful blight.
That sight it left your eye that day.

Stone fired within, anger gone astray.
The sky that shone in eye so bright,
Cannot the dark my days repay.
As stone it flew with all my might.

And so it was, no second sight
To halt it. Neither time to pray!
Through distant time, and long respite
I'm sorrier than I could ever say.

For I never, for that I pay;
In debtors' prison, a thief's plight.
Lacking vision, if hand could stay?
When I turned our day to night.

That look you gave, my inner fright!
My fault my rock plunged into clay.
That look, in turning horrors, requite
The haunted mind unto this very day.
                                    That sight it
left…

One 0' Cock

What the fuck are you waiting for, at one
O' Cock in the morning, cock l' doodle
Doodle do it, she says on the phone, sex
She is fine, and for you; and you, and you!

You alone, Jaded and tied, torn skirts, slick
Thighs, eyes, and bulging, and bulging and I'm
Wishfully willing, poke out my glass eye!
And so, she pokes out both, sucking you dry.

But I'm just watching, voyeuristic phone
Waving, bone shaven imagination,
Immaculate premature ejaculations,
I hear it country-wide, it grinds and groans!

Enslaved to a televised satisfaction
Guarantee of 692223.

The Cross

To be or not to be, expressed question.
Alas poor Jesus, Christ I crossed him.
Fallen am I to experience less Son.
With respect sir your sheep I have lost them.

Beneath Sun nor Moon, my belief, my faith.
Ye hath lost none! Only the Ocean gives
up its time to reign, and rain it willeth.
Giving life to those few, who pray can live?

Amongst wolves, barking and howling for
blood.
Money for talents and the poor be spent.
Double that is due, for Manna the food.
Of love, Ah, to see such a being rent.

Asunder, thunderous side splitting veils
of laughter, verily letting vessels.

Off the Rails

Trax FM, is stuck on repeat
Trax FM, is stuck on repeat
Trax FM is stuck on repeat
Trax FM is stuck on repeat
Trax FM is stuck on repeat
Trax FM is stuck on repeat

Day after day, year after year
Day after day year after year
Day after day, year after year
Day after day, stuck on repeat

Year after year, stuck on repeat
Day after day, stuck on repeat
Year after year, stuck on repeat

Stuck on repeat
Stuck on repeat
Stuck on repeat
Stuck on repeat
Stuck on repeat
Stuck on repeat
Stuck on repeat

Day after day after day after day after day after day after day after day after day after day after day after day after day after day after day aft TODAY OFF!

Memoirs of a Jobseeker

Beginning with Bingham's, a molder by name.
Packing the pattern, again and again;
Punching and scrunching till all feels the same
Sent for a weight, so I wait... It's a game!
Back down the line, flip over the frame,
Splash on the paint, then set it aflame.

Those bridges were burnt, gone up in flames!
We can give you some training, give us your name?
YTS, ITEC; let's put these in frame.
For the National Vocational Qualifications, I gained.
To me and me mates it was all just a game.
I'm Not Very Qualified, so shit stayed the same.

Till I start cleaning windows, it's a job all the same.
At £2.50 an hour my pocket's in flames.
So we signed on the dole, we fiddled the game.
But somethings not right when they called out my name?

They say; "you're defrauding the system for
financial gain!"
So I smile as I say; "It's not me! I've been
framed."

I sign off as I leave, taking me out of the frame,
And onto the windows for more of the same.
So to windows I fell again and again
And to me it has felt like being cast down in
flame
Can I ever, will I ever; wash off the name,
Window Cleaner? "Fuck this for a game!"

Of soldiers: like that is a game!?
Sat in recruitment, do I fit the frame?
Of mind, out of mind, out the door; without
signing my name
I'd rather be skint, than kill, thanks all the same.
So I go out of the door, grab a fag and a flame
And I starting to wonder, what am I doing with
my life yet again?

Warehouses, factories, sales, never say never;
say, never again!
To a life flipping burgers, damn that fat spitting
game.
Too many hopes, dreams; whoppers, cooked in
the flames.

I just want to put pictures in nice funky frames
Paint paintings, sculpt sculptures; print poems,
and more of the same!
To become known as an artist, and be an artist
by name.

To be gainfully free, freed from the frame,
To relinquish the shackles of the game that's the
same,
Perpetually prepared to get pissed down in
flames, this is my art, and Craig Balmer's my
name.

Peace

I believe in peace:
But I see the darkest age of man.
I believe in peace:
When I see the darkness rage in men.
I believe in peace:
But the television says I'm wrong.
I believe in peace:
As death goes reaping through the throngs.
I believe in peace:
When men protest against the strong.
I believe in peace:
When the response to this is bombs.
I believe in peace:
When they respond with locks and chains.
I believe in peace:
When their belief is pain.
Do we believe in peace?
When we sell men the equipment!
Do we believe in peace?
As we profit from every shipment.
Do we believe in peace?
When we side with opposing factions.
Do we believe in peace?
With our gifts of putrefaction.
Do we believe in peace?

When we remotely bomb a church.
Do we believe in peace?
As the entire wedding party burnt!
Do we believe in Peace?
If we cannot admit the error.
Do we believe in peace
When we wage terror against terror.
Can I believe in peace?
As death rains down upon a school.
Can I believe in peace?
When a man can be this cruel!
Can I believe in peace?
When bodies pile up in the street.
Can I believe in peace?
Infant corpses swelling in the heat.
Can I believe in peace?
When ministers preach righteous indignation.
Can I believe in peace?
Religious dedication selling pains
administration.
Can I believe in peace?
When we believe in deaths proliferation.
Can I believe in peace?
When our great hope is nuclear devastation.
You cannot fight for peace.
Paradoxically it's wrong.
You cannot live in peace.
When weapons make you strong.
You can have some peace.

If you'd right what you're thinking.
You can have a piece,
If you walk that way unshrinking.

Extinction Events!

The Sale of the Century
Buy One Get One Free

Look at the cattle!
In their steel and glass houses,
Quietly grazing.

Levelling Up

Whooooaaaarrrrhhhhhhhhhhhhah!
Can you feel it? That levelling up? Feeling,
Let me tell you, I have hit the fiscal ceiling.
That rush of money from back bencher's
pockets,
Spine tingling, hard, in all my anal sockets.

How about you? I am feeling oiled!
Like a rusty spring you just found soiled.
Coiled down that river, liquidity (aw), making
me shiver
Shimmering argent arrow; pulled from a golden
quiver.

A platinum bow shot of majestic precision!
Jubilee Jamboree injection incision,
Into these dark cities, sweaty, vagina's.
Strings of pearls, tossed to the swine herds.

Monkey piss milked from Pidgins' shitter's
Not all that is gold, or diamonds, doth glitters.

Extinction Events!

Absolutely Everything must go
Come on and BOGOF!

It looks like Ethnic's
Cleansing; look how clean
they are becoming?

Placentoid

The dew makes a star!
How they hate you!
The terrible brains,
Dream of a duel they will win inevitably;
Of wars, wars, wars!
Their merciless churn,
Intolerable without mind.
God-bit in him;
The tongues of Hell!
That kill, that kill, that kill.

The dew that flies,
Plummet to their dark address.
Bright as a Nazi lampshade
Against fire and bombs through the roof.
For a minute the sky pours into the hole like
plasma.
The beads of hot metal fly.
The dead bell, the dead bell;
Melts in the wall.
There is no mercy in the glitter of cleavers
After whose stroke the wood rings; echoes
travelling off from the centre like horses.

One cry and I stumble from bed, cow-heavy and floral,
The blood blooms clean.
Stiffens and odours bleed,
The indelible smell.
Smoke rolls and scarves such yellow sullen smokes
I cannot run, I am rooted.
The blood jet is poetry.
And I am aware of my heart: it opens and closes.
The doom mark crawls down the wall,
We have come so far, it is over.

This black boot has no mercy for anybody.
And in truth it is terrible.
Smell the melt of shoe-blacking.
The boot in the face, the brute;
Black sweet blood mouthfuls!
Squelching and squelching through the beautiful red.
The nose, the eye pits, the full set of teeth
But it has no soul, this apparition in a green helmet.
The terrible brains,
The doom mark crawls down the wall.

The sky pours into the hole like plasma.
Now I break up in pieces.
Flesh, bone, there is nothing there.

Then, from the barred yard, the children,
Smell the melt of shoe-blacking,
Old blood of limb stumps.
Empty? Empty. Here is a hand,
A ring of gold with a sun in it?
A cake of soap, a wedding ring, a gold filling.
The blue and red jewels of her rings smoke.

Bombs plummet to their dark address.
Death opened like a black tree, blackly;
So murderous in its strangle of branches.
Their merciless churn, whitens and swallows its
dull stars.
Each dead child coiled, a white serpent.
The air snags and eddies round them.
And this is the fruit of it: Tin white, like arsenic
Their flesh bears no relation.
Bleeding and peeling, touching and melting,
Its snaky acids hiss

Must you kill what you can?
Such coldness, forgetfulness.
The blood jet is poetry bright as a Nazi
lampshade.
Religion drinking the blood blooms clean.
Hiss at my sins, it is a blessing; it is a blessing!
Religion drinking, flickering and pouring, a
pitiful candle.

They can die, I need feed them nothing, I am the owner!

This is the tongue of the dead man: Its snaky acids hiss

Remember, remember his actions. Of snuffed out candle.

Untouched and untouchable, that kill, that kill, that kill!

This work of poetry, a 'cento,' uses the words of Sylvia Plath

Plath, Sylvia. Ariel: Poems by Sylvia Plath, Faber and Faber Limited, 2013, pp. 3-81

Love Mountain

Oh, where art thou? My lady so precious!
Having searched for so long, incoherent, so
blithely.
Is that you that I seek? Can I feel this
cognisance?
Inspired to be witnessed, I come again to this
nexus.
Having walked many roads, most being less
tranquil.
I look now, to the mountains, to seek the
diaphanous!

Fell Queen, of the Water's; Fairest of the Naiad!
The Oread, Diaphanous!
Goddess of boulder and stream, of moss and of
dreams: all that is precious.
Diving through the Moon and the Seas of
Tranquillity.
Lost within oceans, without meaning, and
blithely
Submitting; care free, free flowing from
nexus-to-nexuses.
Submerging complexions dancing within the
ethereal diffractions of a shimmering
cognisance.

Hitherto now I have remained incognito!
Having waded the foulest swamps and traced the
streams, to oblique cascades that plunge beyond
the diaphanous.
Air and graces through the subterranean toward
rivers monstrous; cavernous inexplicable
nexuses.
An explorer, a forager, for a pearl that's most
precious.
Mysterious to most and if considered; quite
blithely!
Unfathomed Oceanographer of the
Most-High-Seas: Perilous yet tranquil.

Seeks passage: Tranquillity is Buffeted,
blustered, and blown, by blunt scythe cyclones,
tranquil,
Rainbow and butterfly chasers alight upon the
Wainwritten hills. Cognisant,
Or otherwise engaging themselves with blithe
Enthusiasms for those diaphanous
Robes of understanding; of waters less tangible,
more than incredible: Precious!
Cleansing, knocking it out of the Shakespearean
Heartlands and into the next nexus.

Of beauty: Worthy; only to the finest of
sculptors, of filigree beyond every nexus.

Every possibility! Every curve: Enthralled, wild
tranquillity.
By design? Or God given lustre? Either road,
equally precious.
A Masters stroke of Lord riven genius;
Cognisance
Unfurled, and beyond the pale of the opaquest
truths or diaphanous
Undertakings. A Miraculous Conception!
Blithely

Meandering as they were back down this
mountain toward callipygian tapestries. Blithe
Chattering's, friends amongst themselves,
looking now for an exit or nexus.
No further perambulations are required. As the
Sun sets on this scene, and the night falls behind
us: Diaphanous,
Tranquil.
No need of cognisance.
And so, all the more precious.

Quiet now Sestina, relax, be blithe, become
tranquil.
You have reached the lasting nexus. We're
alighting upon the campfires of cognisance!
Diaphanous fragrances warp and waft, weft and
weave across amber-lit faces to the sounds of

gentle harmonic phrases. "More wine please!"
The subtle sweetness's of kisses, and precious,
very precious little left to say.

Pygmalion

The words touched a heart, 'twas cold as stone.
They lay in languish, never given language.
No air carved with tongue or spoke to assuage.
Lifeless form within; encaged of bone.

A hearth unlit, within an empty home.
No pulsing flames for poor soul to engage
In warmth; relieve that speech from languid
State, in darkened cave of loves dethrone.

No words that return from set marbled lips.
No echo coming back from the heart abyss.
No God heard his awkward prayer.
Aphrodite' refrain, the candles amiss?!
Pygmalion falls in the temple; he slips
Toward loveless death; and stones, they cry
despair.

Extinction Events!

If You Break It! You buy it!
Buy One Get One Free!

One point five'n rising.
Conservatives plant Rosebank.
What a good idea!
Go! Get back to your grazing.
Now, what is for tea, my dear?